WORKING

(I Do It For The Money)

WORKING

(I Do It For The Money)

By Bill Owens

Simon and Schuster / New York

Published by Simon and Schuster
A Division of Gulf & Western Corporation
Simon & Schuster Building
Rockefeller Center
1230 Avenue of the Americas
New York, New York 10020

Designed by/Catherine Flanders/Graphic Design /San Francisco
Manufactured in the United States of America

1 2 3 4 5 6 7 8 9 10

Library of Congress Cataloging in Publication Data

Owens, Bill.
Working.

1. Labor and laboring classes — United States — 1970- — Pictorial works. 2. Professions — United States — Pictorial works. I. Title.
HD8072.09 301.44'4'0973 77-2013
ISBN 0-671-22820-x
ISBN 0-671-22782-3 Pbk.

The author would like to thank Rosemary Nightingale for her invaluable editorial assistance.

When I meet someone for the first time, my initial question is "What do you do for a living?" It's an acceptable way of asking "Who are you?" The answer allows me to make certain assumptions not only about that person's life-style but also about their background, their education, their opinions, their dreams and aspirations. Immediately we have something to talk about, but more important, I know whom I'm talking to.

As a photographer for a suburban newspaper I was exposed to the small business community. Fascinated by the variety of work situations around me, I decided to investigate the larger business, industrial and agricultural communities. I wanted to find out how people feel about their work, how important it is in their lives, whether they view their job as the source of their identity.

The project took me to many parts of California and across the United States. I soon discovered that I had set myself no easy task. Many companies have their own photographers and are unwilling to admit outsiders. Some companies suspected that I might be an industrial spy, others were committed to work schedules and feared that I would distract workers and slow production. To those who refused me access, there is no second time around. Sorry you didn't understand. To everyone who cooperated and asked for nothing in return, thanks.

September 1976

Bill Owens

WORKING

I've been a UPI correspondent, a publicist for an Italian film producer, a writer for the U.S. Army, a public relations man and an operations manager for record stores. Now I'm promotion and marketing director for a newspaper chain. Within a year, I'll be off to Turkey. It will be a jumping-off place. The world will be my oyster.

I'm a member of "Who's Who in Credit." In 1958 I was one of three people who worked on the development of the bank credit card. Today thirty-four million people use that card. I've worked with people who made things happen. It's helped me develop as a person.

I really enjoy being here because it's my pleasure to help people. They'd have to fire me before I'd quit. I know I'm loved and vice versa.

I'm an electrical-cable splicer working for a public utility. I earn $356 a week, which is more than adequate. Today everyone is complaining about their gas and electricity bills. It's not my fault if your bill is $120 because you're heating a swimming pool. I believe in conservation and do what I can.

There's no substitute for experience. It takes eight to ten years to become a drug-store manager. You have to start at the bottom as a clerk. At our weekly meetings, we decide what items our stores will carry, what advertisements to place, and discuss operational problems.

Ziriya
Sunken Treasure
CHOPPER STRIKE
SKY COPTER
HOLLY HOBBIE
REFRIGERATOR FREEZER
PIN BALL GAME
CrackerJack
THE GAME OF
A FAMILY GAME
safe
HOLLY HOBBIE
TELSTAR
FINGER PAINT
airtrix
MOSTLY GHOSTLY
SCOOBY DOO
SURE FLYER
woodburning

Like everybody else, I'm caught up in the rat race. I work eighty hours a week and with my real-estate investments earn $100,000 a year. I just got divorced. In the insurance business the public thinks we promise the moon but we can only deliver half a moon.

MEDALLION OF HONOR
FIREMARK
AWARD

Being a receptionist is a catch-all job; you do everything. Mostly we're dealing with salesmen and they like to see young women. I've stayed here six years because I got married and my husband didn't want me to commute to a better-paying job.

I'm the mayor of the city and a practicing pathologist. I've won ten of the twelve public offices I've run for and I've never found a career I've enjoyed more. This year I ran for the United States Senate but I didn't make it.

FUND
KC
OF THE WORLD

As a theoretical physicist I generally don't tell people what I do. It's useless explaining because unless you know about the subject it's mysticism. Some of my mathematical problems take a year or more to solve. I carry them around with me. So really I'm working all the time, even when I'm in bed.

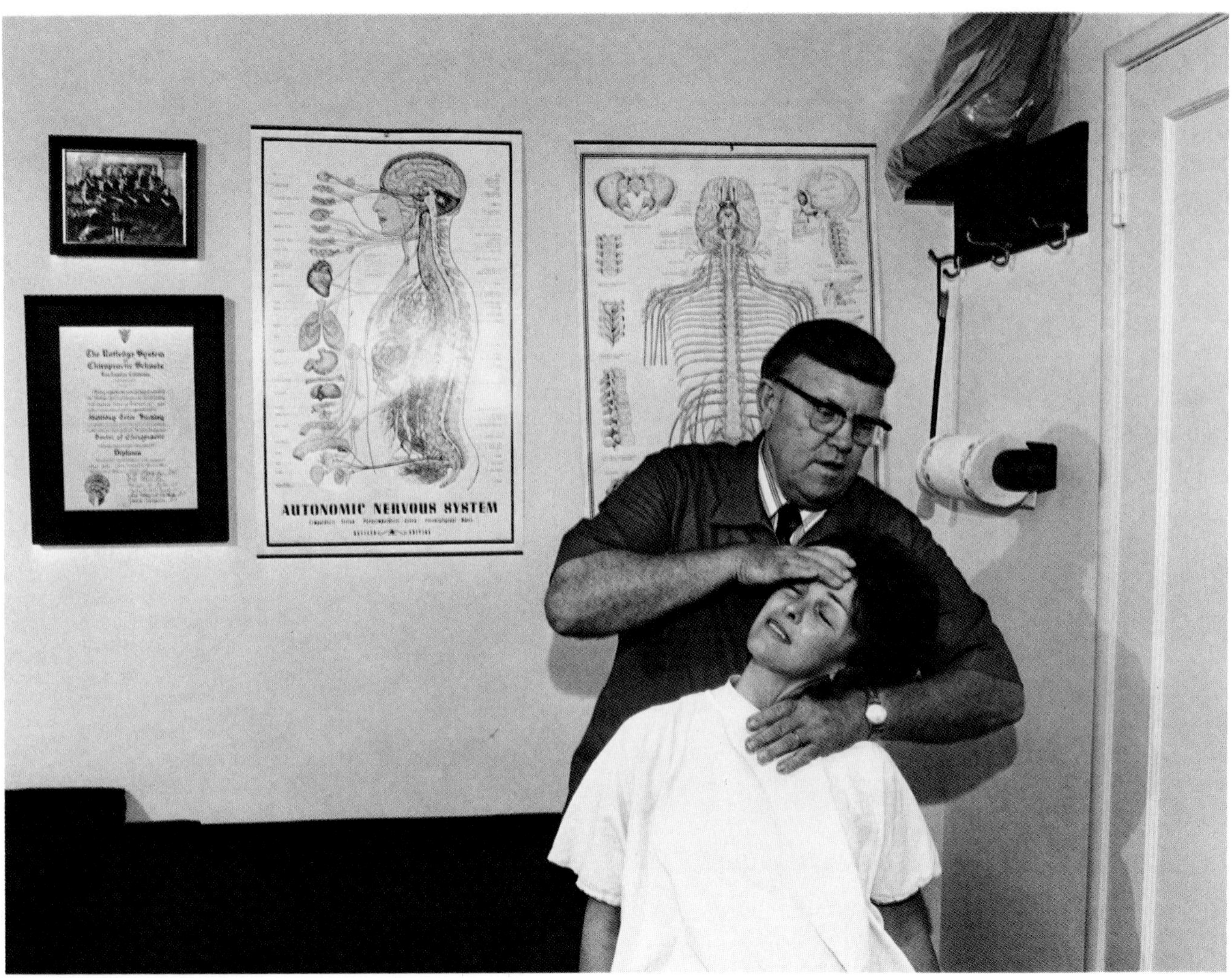

I've been a chiropractor for thirty-three years, working directly and indirectly with nerves through the spinal column. I'm thinking of retiring in a couple more years and going into worm farming. Worms are an asset to society.

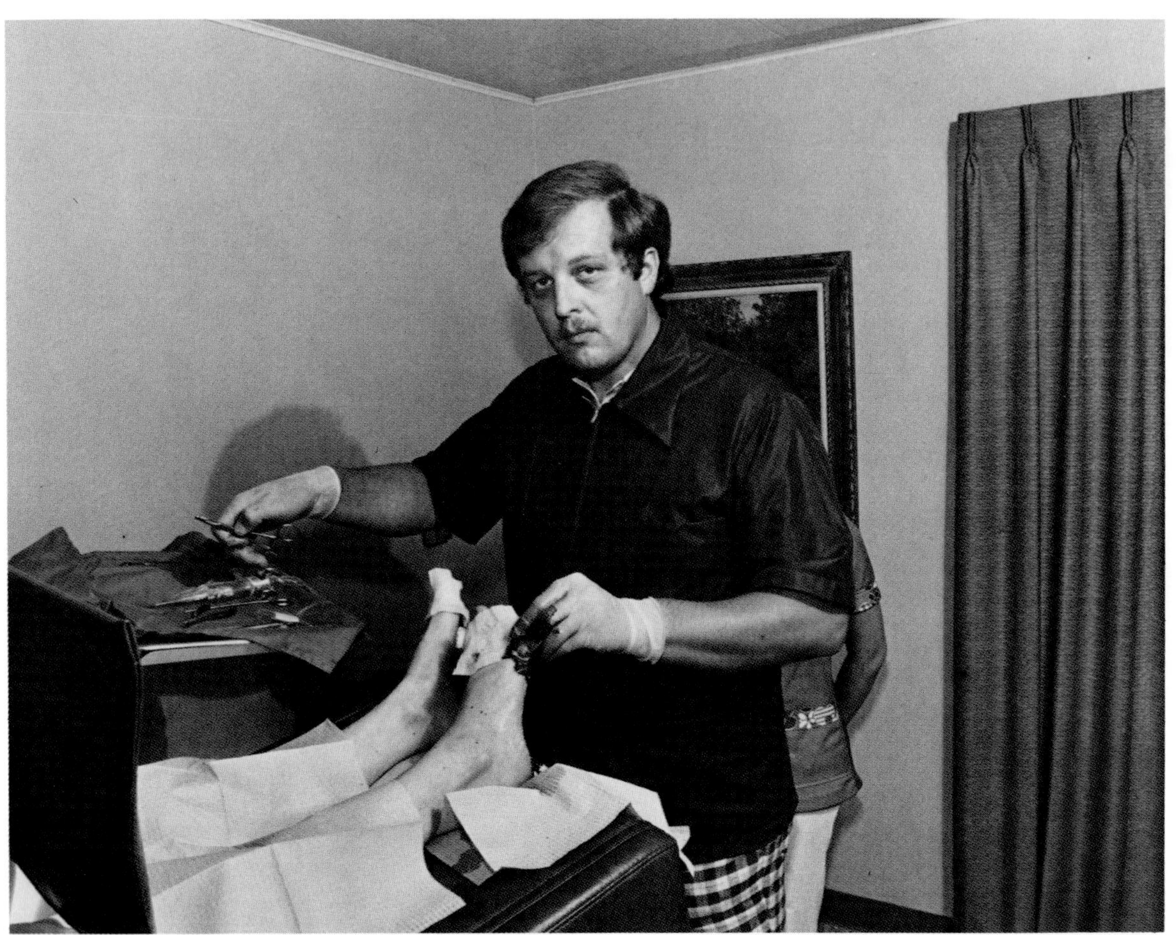

At one time or another, 70 percent of people have a foot problem but only 3 percent seek professional care. I enjoy being a podiatrist. To see a patient who has suffered with corns for years and to correct that problem is a gratifying experience. When your feet hurt, you hurt all over.

I'm a new-realist painter. People think it's glamorous to paint but it's just hard work. Each painting takes two to four months to complete. The possibility of getting national acclaim is almost nil.

I've been a hooker for five years. How else could I support myself and my daughter by working a few hours? To be a good hooker you have to be warm to a total stranger. You need technique, personality and the ability to communicate with the john. If I had to choose between a man and a typewriter, I'd take a man every time.

I was a lawyer before I became a private detective. This is a more interesting way of making a living. I've been in the business for more than twenty years now and have worked on just about every case imaginable.

Our peanut butter and jelly sandwiches are frozen and shipped across the nation to schools, convalescent homes and hospitals. Because of mass production we can manufacture a sandwich cheaper than you can make one at home.

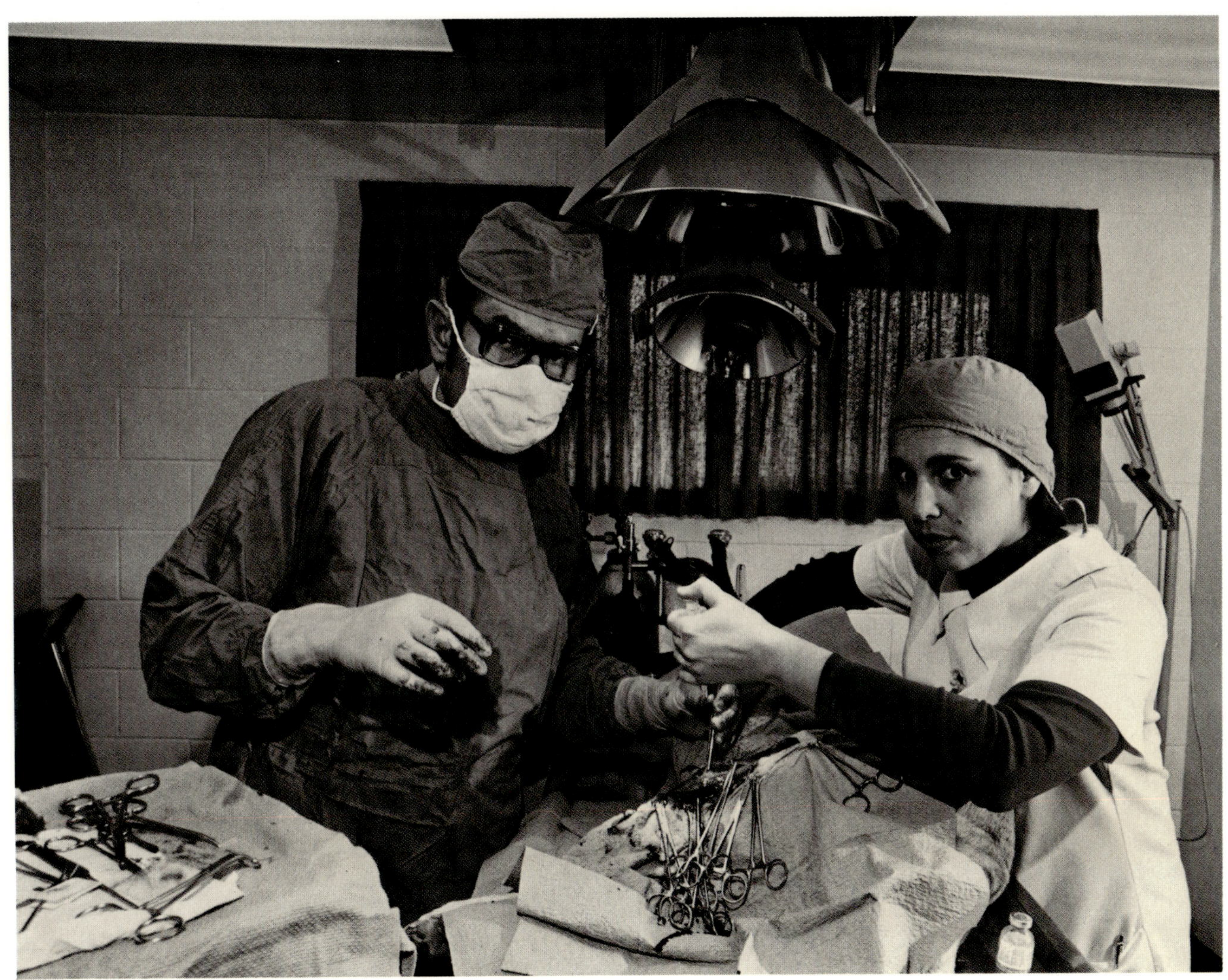

When I was a kid I dreamed of being a veterinarian. Today's pets are practically family members. It's not like the old days when animals were left to die. I'm operating on a ten-year-old dog for a torn knee ligament, an injury football players often get.

I don't want to retire tomorrow. I enjoy what I'm doing as a junior-college instructor in mathematics. Today's students aren't as dedicated as they used to be. Life is more complex and there are more distractions. Nowadays a lot of my students are housewives. They don't have any goals; they just want to learn.

I own my own pharmacy and work sixty to seventy hours a week. I don't do it for the money. The gratification is in helping people and being part of the community. I could make more money working for a drugstore chain, but if I did it for the dollar I'd become a cruel and hardened person.

Armour Thyroid

NO SMOKING

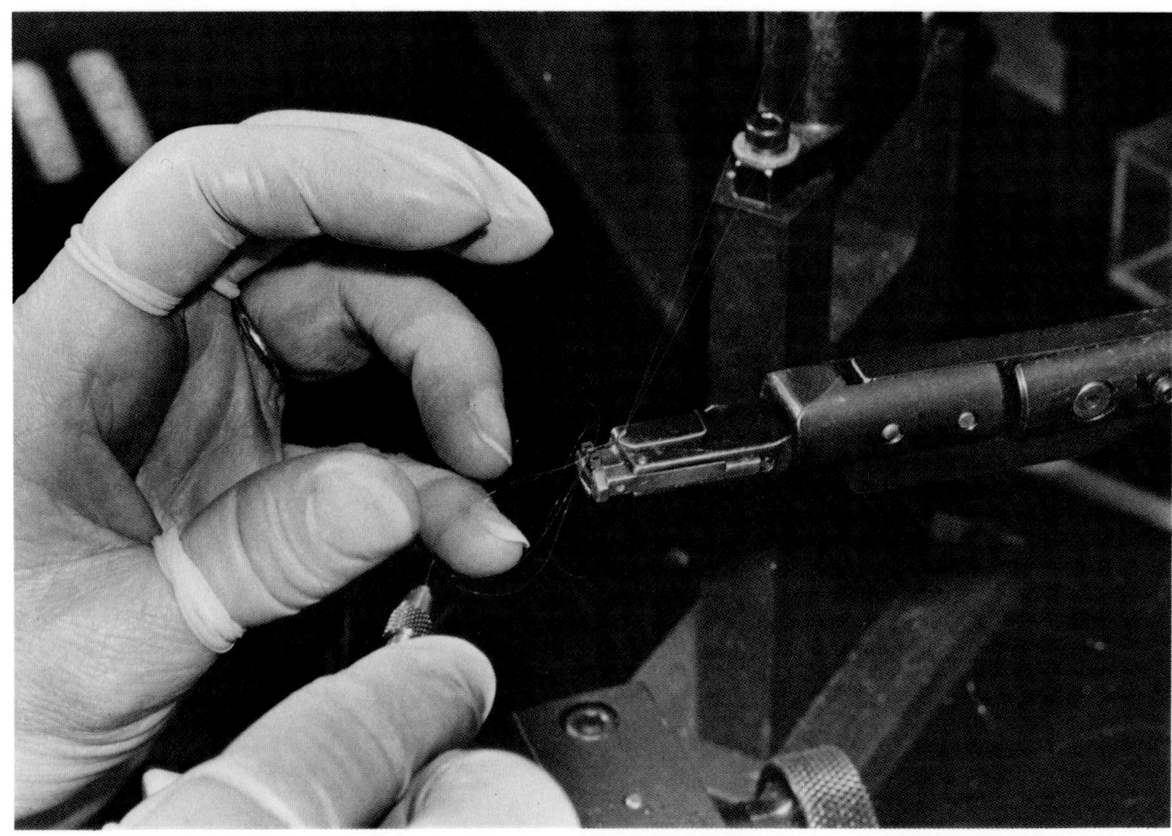

Men don't have the patience to become coil winders. This job has lots of tension.
Each day is a challenge and you have to learn to relax, otherwise you can break a wire.
It took me three weeks to wind my first thirteen loops. These coils are part of a computer recording head.

The space shuttlecraft is a 2.7-billion-dollar manned space vehicle. It will have the capacity to carry thirty tons of material into orbit. Someday it will place solar collection panels in outer space to beam energy back to earth.

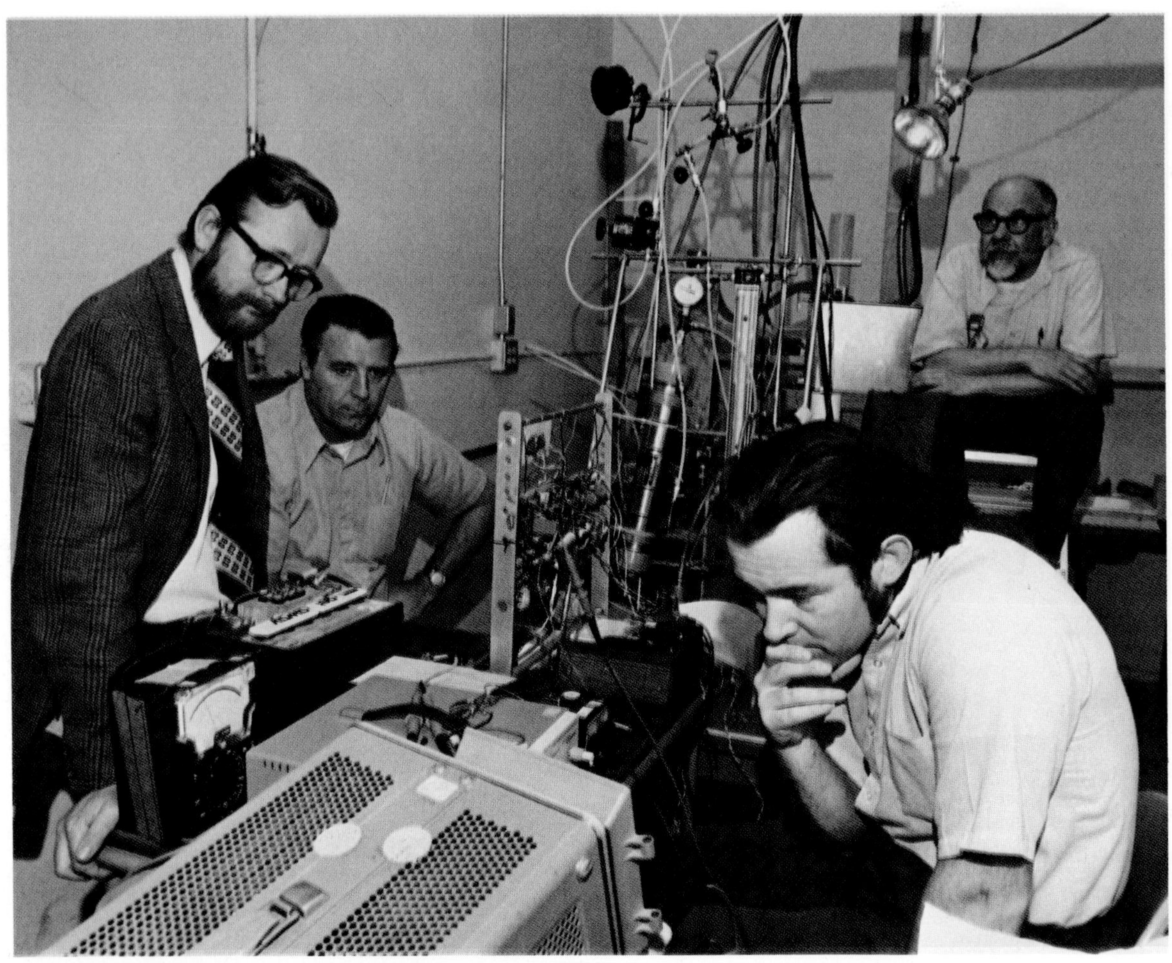

Our interdisciplinary engineering group has been working on the heart-assistance pump for seven years. I'd rather be working on the fuel-injection pump for cars and trucks which operates on the same principle.

My dream is to be an airline stewardess, but I'm not old enough. In the meantime I operate a pneumatic tie-wrap gun and make harnesses for electronic pong games. I can't wait until I turn twenty-one.

For forty-three years I've worked as a dental technician. You have to satisfy each individual patient, yet run a small production line to get the work done. Nobody gets rich making something with his own hands. I'd have liked to have been in manufacturing, insurance or real estate on a large scale. I'd have done it for the money.

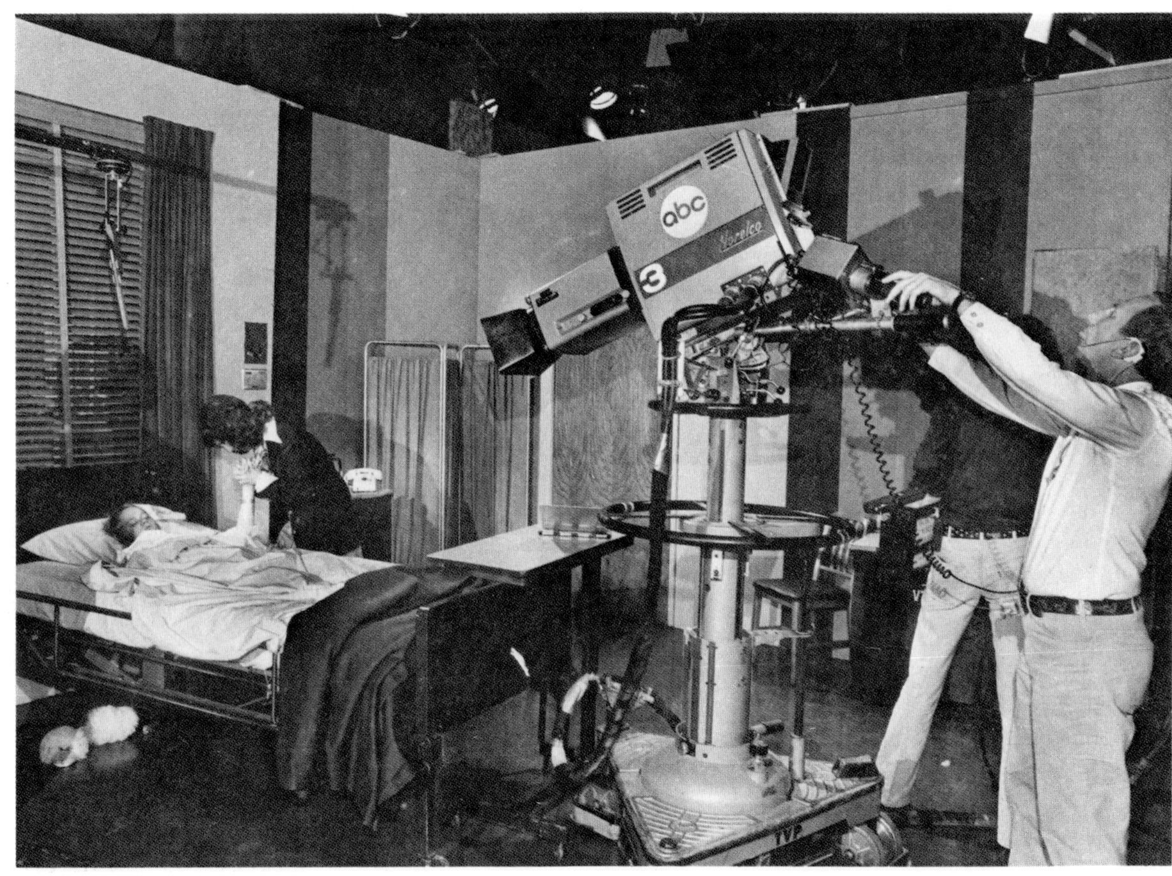

Daytime soap opera has one purpose — to sell laxatives, fast food and vitamins. Our audience is women who sit at home worrying about their health and their family. We provide escapism.

The capital market is based on government-issued bonds. Our office trades fifty to a hundred million dollars' worth of government and corporate securities each day. This can be an ulcer business but it's an opportunity to make an abnormal amount of money. It gives me the means for dreams to become realities.

OPEN BALL TEST

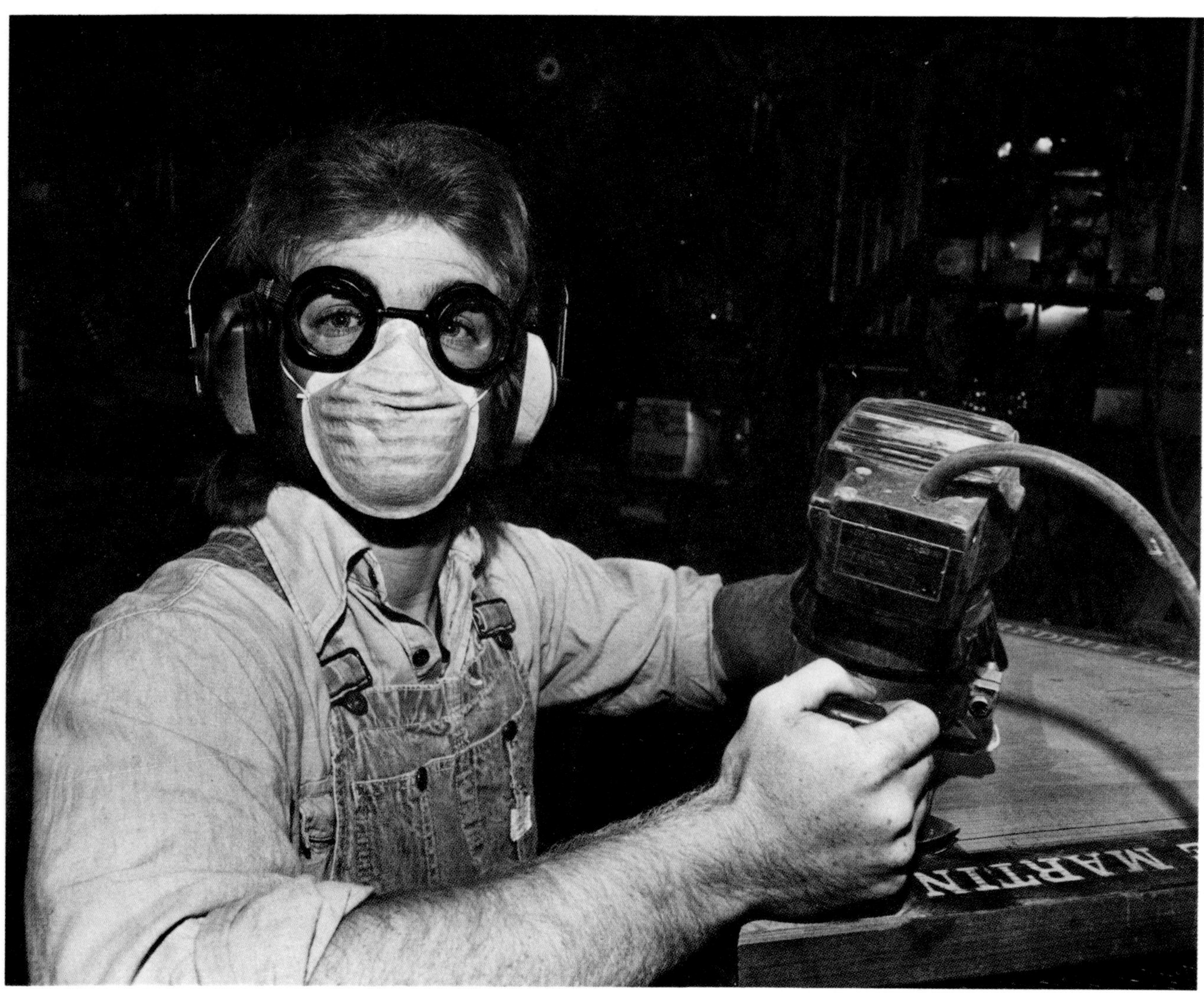

I tried college for a couple of weeks but I had a family to support so I went back to work for my dad. I've been carving signs since I was fourteen years old.

I work with computerized techniques, studying plant and animal cells. Someday we hope to genetically manipulate animals, eliminating disease and selecting features which will make them more efficient. I know of only four people in the world doing this work.

It takes a year to make a gyro-ball guidance system for the C-5A aircraft. It's not a hard job physically, but you have to program yourself to keep the stress down, otherwise you'll climb the walls. I'm going to retire at fifty-five and go back to the mountains and grow vegetables.

I'm a newspaper city editor. Hollywood made editors seem glamorous and powerful, but times have changed. Now reporters have more fun. There aren't many dummies in this business. It's a labor of love.

I'm a cloth cutter and it takes eight hours to cut the pockets for 120 pairs of pants. It takes two hours to cut the pants. Once you get the hang of it, it's easy. On the weekends I earn almost as much money playing guitar in a Latin rock-and-roll group.

I've worked part-time ever since the seventh grade. It's a waste to sit around. As a wash boy, I earn $40 a week, which isn't bad for a high-school student. I spend the money on my truck and my girl friend.

Part of my job as a waiter is to be a zoo-runner. We carry the huge dish of ice cream around the tables while other waiters beat a drum. Then we deliver the ice-cream zoo to the table having the party.

On our commune, everyone has to work. We chase off the freeloaders. The commune has to make money. It has to be a business, then it can grow. The government isn't going to take care of you. You have to band together to help each other.

My wife and I don't like the term "head shop."
We are in the youth-oriented business.
In seven years we have never been hassled by
the police. We don't use drugs; we want
to protect our livelihood.

I've always been sales-oriented. If I can sell myself, I can sell the product. I take pride in my customers and have sold nine cars to one family. Everyone you meet is different.

I'm a wilderness-equipment designer and create environmental living-space. To me, work and play are the same thing. My life allows total freedom of expression. For example, I just designed an outdoor shower for my boyfriend.

In four years as an employment counselor, I have only placed one woman in management — as a trainee. As a feminist I find this disgusting. Women make up 53 percent of our planet and it's time the world started paying attention to our potential. People work to maintain their sanity.

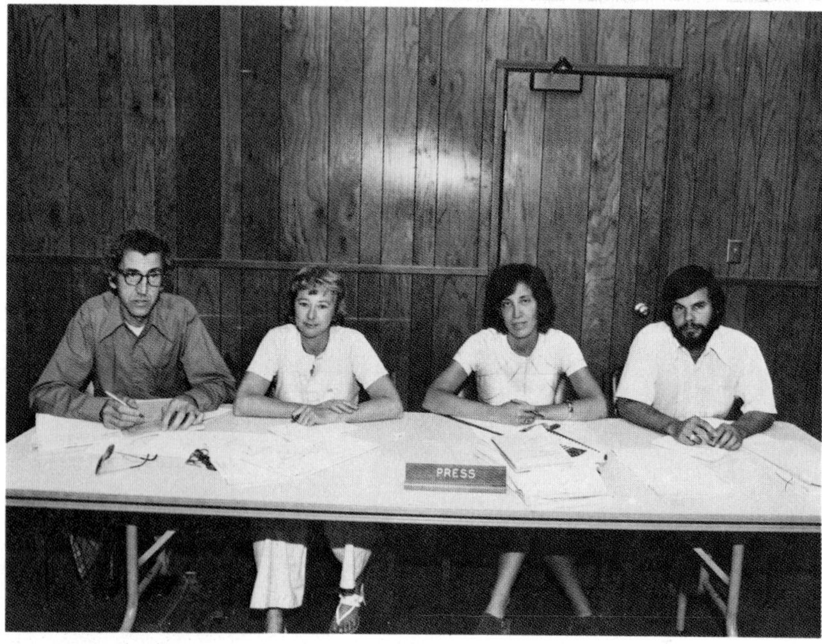

Being a reporter is a responsible job. You funnel information to the community. I like to be where the action is, where decisions are made that affect people's lives. From one city council meeting, four reporters will write four different stories about the same subject.

I'm a philanthropist. Each year, depending on the stock market, I give away up to $500,000. On my income tax forms I call myself a political maverick. I give money to political candidates, institutions and liberal politicians who support arms control and population control.

The New York Times

The tax system is for the rich. As a CPA you have to be careful. If I give bad advice, I'm liable. The government should provide information that the average person can understand. Most people just can't read the forms.

Being a salesman is easy. It's fun to manipulate people, to get a reaction, to find out where they're at. I used to be in management; I hated it. All I want to do is sell furniture.

24

I used to be a chef and my partner was a garbage foreman. He was making $107 a week and going crazy. Now we sell apples and oranges from the back of a pickup truck. You meet people of every race — rich and poor, doctors and dentists. Everyone loves good fruit. We're making a living and enjoying ourselves.

The Any Timer

You have to be in good physical condition in the fence business because it's hard work. Everybody in the business is related, either your brother or your cousin works for us or for another fence company. Our product is better than the customer expects. We use the best materials and do the job right.

Our dress manufacturing business started in a kitchen seven years ago. Today we have fifty employees and this year we'll ship five-million dollars' worth of dresses. Our company is multiracial. We have blacks, whites, Filipinos, Chinese, Chicanos — you name it, we got it.

Old Fashioned Soda
Sundaes
Floats
Cones
Dip Cones
ROYAL TREATS
Sundae Supreme
Banana Split
Fiesta Sundae
Par Fay
Short Cake
Blizzard
Buster Bar
Curly Top Cone
Misty Kiss
TAKE HOME
Pints
Quarts
½ Gallon
Novelties
Mr. Misty qt.

A banana split has one banana, three lumps of ice milk, crushed pineapple, strawberries, chocolate syrup and whipped cream. In two days of our forty-nine-cent special we sold five thousand splits. Businessmen want a pretty face at the counter and counter girls have to have personality to deal with the public.

It takes a lot of brains to be a model. You're not just a body with a pretty face. You have to have the latest salable look and be a self-starter with drive and energy. It's a lot of fun meeting artistic people and going on location. It's something different.

This is the only gold dredge in the continental United States. It operates around the clock, seven days a week, moving three million cubic yards of sand and gravel every year. The dredge makes twenty-five cents per cubic yard and with the depressed gold market sometimes doesn't break even.

I'm a supervisor for a drayage company and tonight we're moving an oil-derrick platform. It's 116 feet long and weighs 186 tons. It will take us three hours to go six miles. I don't think I could work sitting at a desk. My next job will be moving oil-refinery equipment in Saudi Arabia.

Being a mechanic is all I've ever known. I started when I was fifteen years old and have done it ever since — except when I drove a tank for General Patton in World War II. I'm my own boss and take in the jobs I want. A good mechanic is never out of work.

I'm a rear-bumper securer. I do forty-five bumpers an hour and have had the same job for eleven years. This is a very impersonal place to work. If you had a heart attack they'd replace you in two minutes. Never fall down in front of the line, they'd run it over you. I make $300 a week but it takes a certain type of person to do this job.

Forty years ago I left the farm in Minnesota because it was hard work. I'm now an aircraft mechanic. When you have to work — well this is it.

I'm a train conductor. I love railroading, it's exciting. Each trip is different and I never know where I'm going. My dad and his brothers, my wife, her dad and her brothers were all railroaders. It runs in the family.

I'm a plastics molder and make oven doors for airline kitchenettes. I could never work indoors where I can't see the sun. I've been thinking about women's lib. Maybe I'll join something and do volunteer work. Maybe someday I'll work with children.

I've been skating since I was ten years old and have been a professional skater for nineteen years. In figure skating you deal with the inner self. Like ballet it involves discipline, choreography, heartbreak and finally a sense of accomplishment. Women take this class to stay in shape.

In thirty-one years as a ladleman I've never been injured. I won't take promotion to pit boss because I have a lot of responsibility right here in this handle. It controls 150 tons of molten steel. I like it here. I don't bother nobody and nobody bothers me. It's just a job.

I'm unemployed and haven't worked in six years. Whenever I apply for a job I fail the physical. I had my spine fused in a back operation, lost my right heel in a bike accident, got an ulcer and had 80 percent of my stomach removed, and got shot three times in the Bay of Pigs invasion. I've lived a good life. I wouldn't change it.

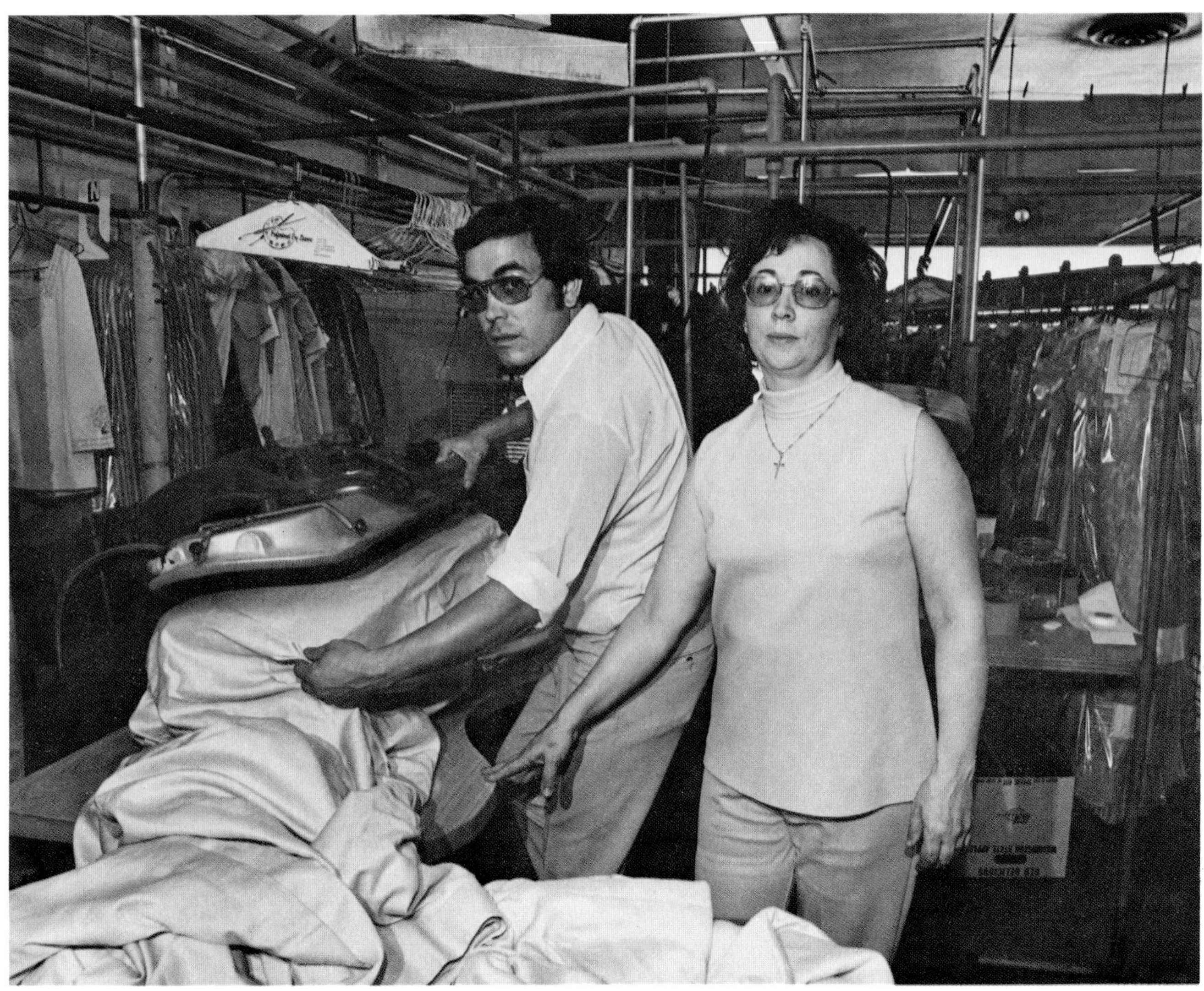

America is the best country in the world. In the Azores we'd go to the movies and America would seem like a dream. We came here with fifty dollars in our pocket and worked twelve hours a day, six days a week to save money to buy this dry-cleaning business. America is better than we thought. We have everything we ever wanted.

We're the last of the gandy dancers or track gangs. All track-laying today is completely automated. The railroad doesn't need people, it needs machines. Gangs used to sing all day and pull their pincher bars on a particular word. We just pull on numbers.

Fishing is the only thing the Indians have left. Nobody complains about netting millions of fish in the ocean but if an Indian nets twenty-five salmon in a river it's a crime. I give away most of my fish to the old Indians in the mountains and log nine months of the year. Like everyone else, I'm divorced. If I don't meet my payments, I'll go to jail.

I make nine dollars an hour operating a fence-weaving machine. I used to be a policeman at the same salary but with four kids I wanted a job where I'd be home evenings. It was hard to give up the security of police work but now my wife and I are happy because I have a regular job with regular hours.

Being a hot-man is super hard work and super dangerous. On a commercial roofing job, a good hot-man can make $80 to $100 a day. That's if he gets any overtime.

It can take six months or more of on-the-job training to become a microelectronics assembly technician. Only young people can do this work as your eyes don't last. The circuit I'm working on is part of a guidance system for military aircraft. I ride horses and play tennis to relieve the tension.

As the plant manager, I find the development of the hydro harvester a real challenge. It's a four-thousand-dollar environmental chamber, which sprouts and grows cereal grains like wheat and barley. It can produce 360 pounds of grass a day and will be used in the future because land will cost too much.

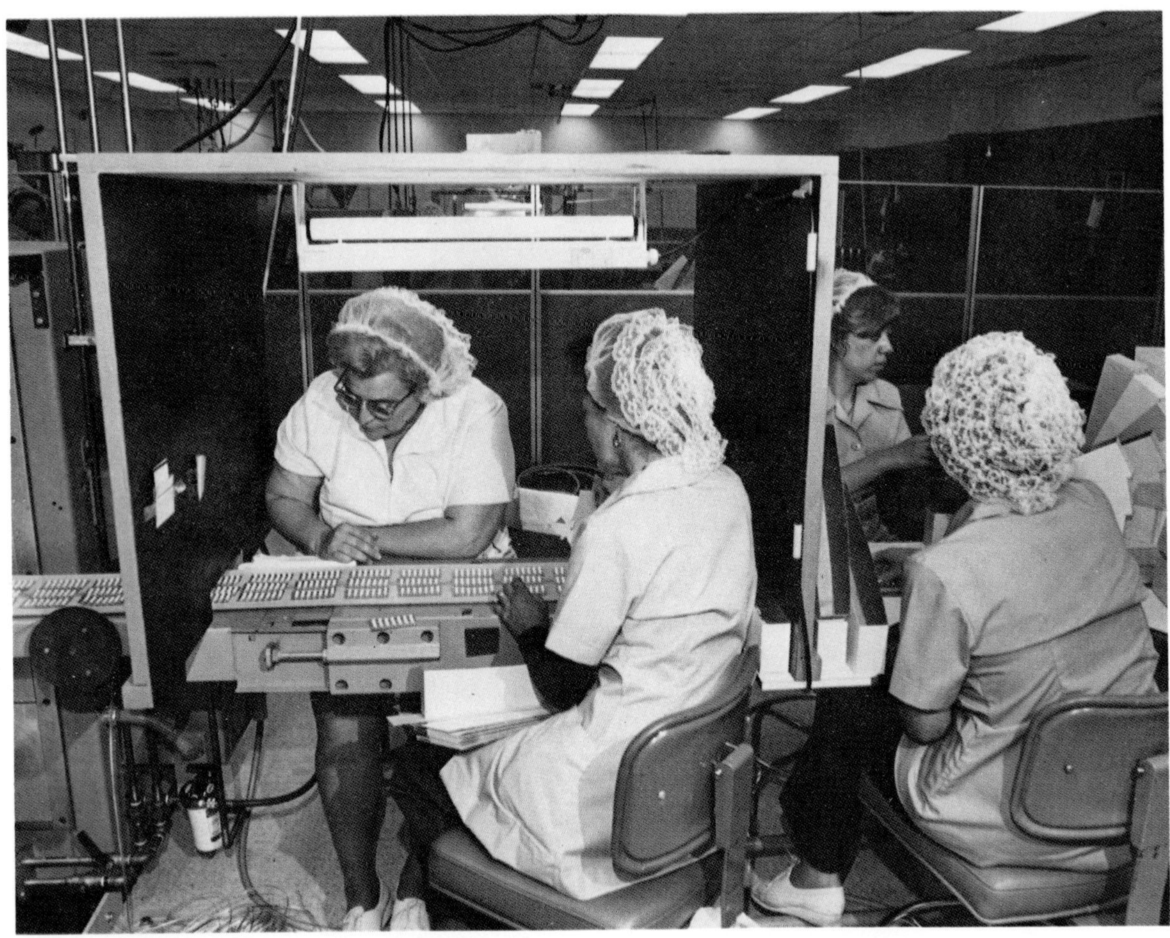

I'm a table worker inspecting birth control pills. After working here for two years, I can't believe there are any babies being born anywhere. My husband is a minister. When your kids go to college you need the money, so here I am.

Baking is the oldest trade in the world. We believe in customer satisfaction and start baking at 1:30 in the morning to ensure freshness. If it's mass-produced, you have to take it or leave it.

Television cameramen are a special breed. When you read something in a book you say that's someone's opinion. When you see it on TV you say that's gospel. I have one minute, thirty seconds to make a statement. It has to be accurate, it has to be the truth.

I'm a mother and a waitress. I enjoy what I'm doing but wouldn't want to do it for a lifetime. I'm divorced and find it difficult to meet men who want to have a relationship. Someday I'd like to go back to school.

As a union carpenter I earn $90 a day. That includes my medical, dental and retirement program. I can only work like this for about ten years before I'm burnt out or injured. I want to be foreman next — more money for less work.

union
VICEROY
51
HILTON INNS
AL UNSER
VICEROY
5
HILTON
Valvoline
VICEROY

We can package 50,000 torpedo sandwiches a day. You don't think about the line, you just do your work over and over again. Almost everyone who works here came from Mexico. It's their first job in America.

Sports-car racing is dominated by men in their forties because sponsors don't like to risk a hundred-thousand-dollar car in the hands of an unproven driver. Most drivers are really guinea pigs and more get killed testing cars than racing them. The car is really a 200-mph billboard for the sponsor.

Everyone's garbage looks the same. When I started in the business seven years ago, I thought the smell was going to get to me. Someday this area will provide land for four homes and pasture for horses and cows.

I'm a refugee from China. I sew pockets on pants. Every day I have work, and living here is easy. In China it's hard to find a job. Someone has to recommend you. I don't speak English and I'm too old to learn so I'll never get a better job.

Hand-rolling cigars is a work of art, which most of us learned as kids in Cuba. We're on piecework and each of us can roll about 600 cigars a day.

I don't think of glassblowing as work even though it has all the aspects of being a business. I work fifty to sixty hours a week. If I don't like what I make I can throw it away or melt it down.

Our twenty-cylinder diesel engine was originally designed for ships. Now it is used in the backup system for a nuclear reactor. It takes a year from design to final delivery. The engine has to make 300 consecutively successful starts, each within ten seconds, before it can be installed in a reactor.

I've been a sandblaster for twenty years. It's not hard work. In ten years I'll retire. I don't know what I'm going to do then.

WATERBEDS

I gross over $200,000 a year as the owner-manager of a donut store, but there's a price to pay. I come to work at 2:00 A.M. to begin the daily routine of making 250 dozen donuts. I eat dinner at 4:00 in the afternoon and am in bed by 7:30. I was a Depression baby. Now kids say there has to be something better.

When my health got bad I quit the dry-cleaning business and started playing rhythm and blues full time. Nobody can play my style. I use a double pick, one on my finger and one on my thumb. If I had my health, I'd go back into the cleaning business.

A plant serviceman cleans, trims, prunes, waters and exchanges rented plants. I'm dusting a fiddle-leaf fig plant at the Trans-America building observation floor. I'm totally content with what I'm doing for now.

I'm one of the first freak fishermen on the West Coast. It's a life-style rather than a living. I want to conserve natural energy by doing more with less, so I sell the crabs I catch directly to people. Money is a paper signature for energy.

You have to be a little goofy to be in this business. To cook every day, you have to be a psychologist and an artist. I enjoy cooking and I like to eat. If you don't like it, don't serve it.

I've taught my baton class through all my pregnancies. The exercise has been good for me. I didn't close my baton studio because there'd be forty girls without a teacher.

I make $142 a week trimming and inspecting rubber tiles used to soundproof nuclear submarines. On a good day I can trim 1,000 tiles. Six years ago I came from Portugal. In my country I was a nurse. In America I needed to work but couldn't qualify as a nurse.

The main thing about being a barber is that someday you'll meet someone who'll get you out of the business. A barber has no benefits. To make it, your wife has to work. The good thing is the freedom. You can say what you like to your customers and on a slow day you can play golf.

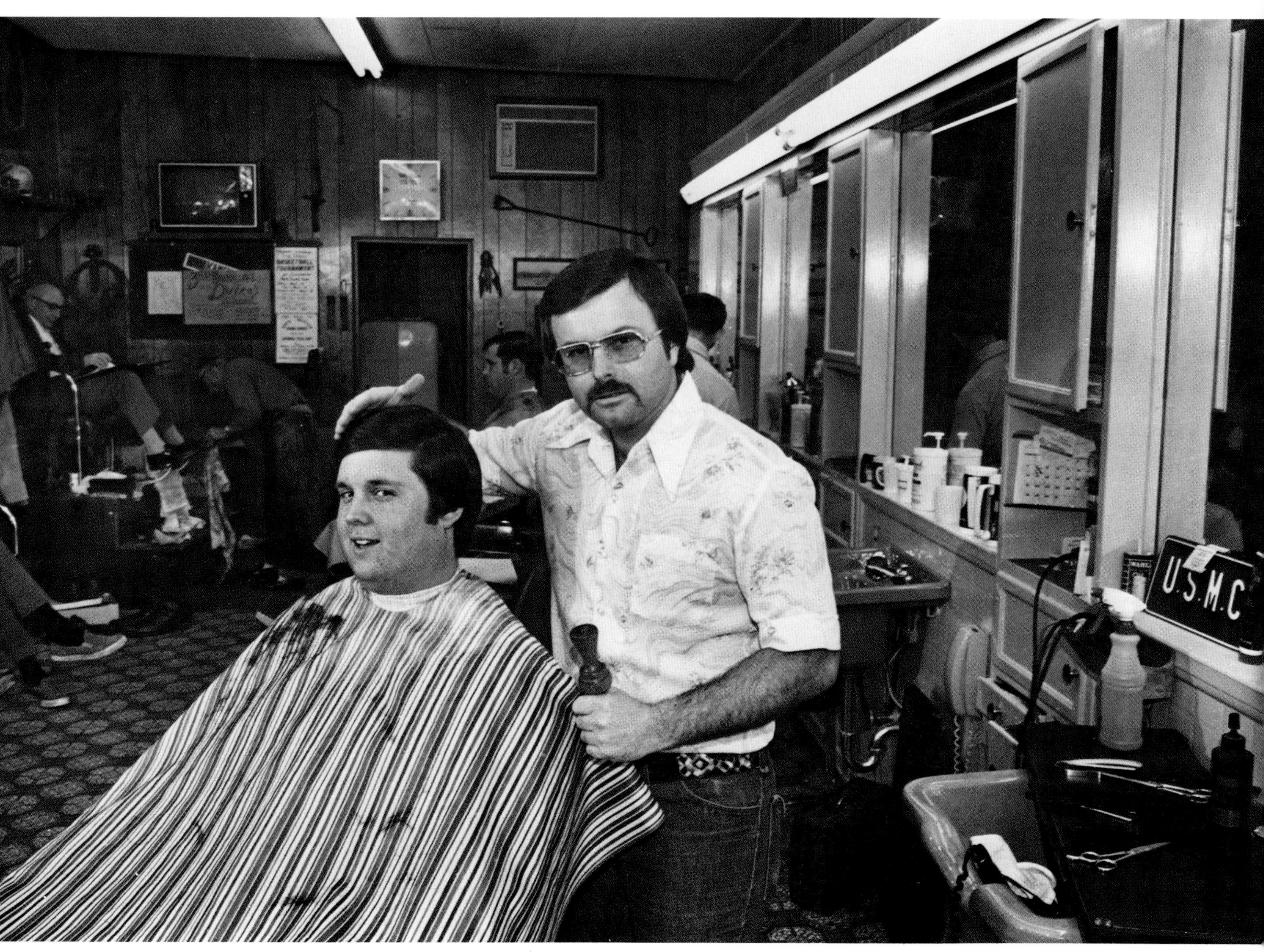
U.S.M.C

NO GAINS
WITHOUT

EXTRA! EXTRA! EXTRA!
SAN FRANCISCO GLOBE
TWO CAMERA 35 EDITORS FLY TO TOKYO ON PAN AM
EXTRA! EXTRA! EXTRA!
SAN FRANCISCO GLOBE
EAT YOUR HEART OUT ARTHUR GOLDSMITH

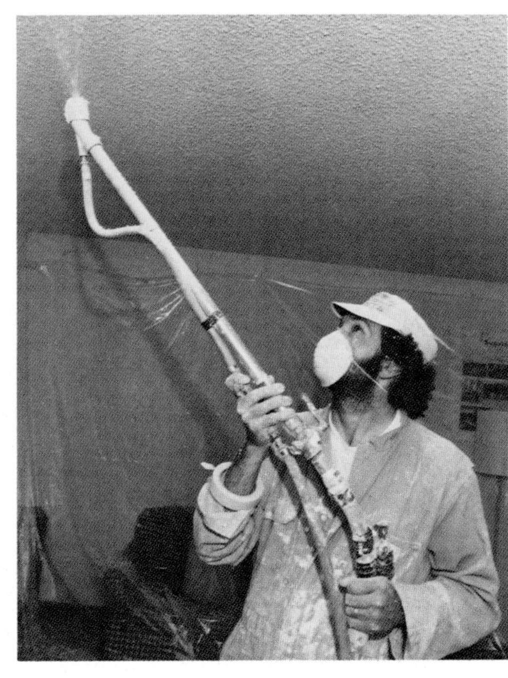

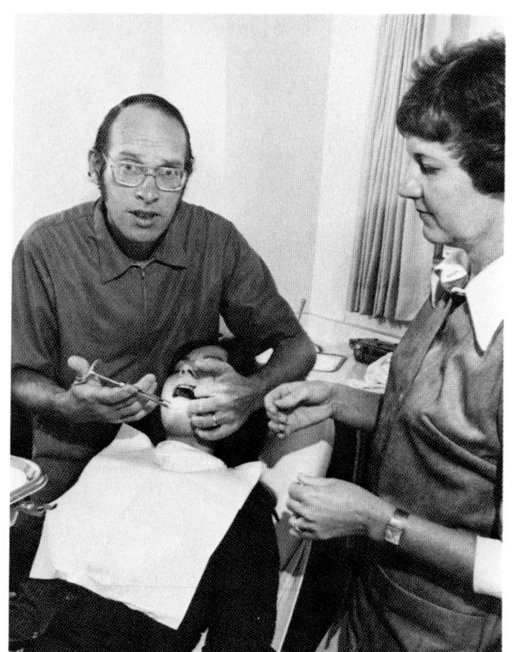

I like working at the shelter workshop. I can be productive and be part of the community. I make money and pay my own way. On my days off I watch TV, ride my bike and write letters to my friends. Someday I'm thinking of getting married.

I've been a shoe salesman for thirty-six years. The way people take care of their shoes shows their character. Seventy percent of people wear shoes that don't fit. When you sell good merchandise it doesn't come back but the people do.

Our grandfather started the redwood tank business in 1902. There's still nothing to beat redwood tanks for water storage. They're cheap to build and maintenance free. Today the hot tub is big business. The new leisure class installs a tub in the back yard to entertain company.

The only way to learn anything in photography is by making lots of mistakes. It's a painful education. Photography's a wonderful hobby but a very difficult business.

save the jetty

WALT DISNEY
0
LIMITED
Alice

Milking is a 365-days-a-year job. Our milk hands sleep three to four hours between shifts and get four days off a month. Usually they stay on the ranch. Most of them don't speak English. We give them a house, electricity, $625 a month and free milk.

Being a grain broker is the old "buy 'em low, sell 'em high" game. After the one o'clock bell, brokers have fifteen minutes to close their market orders. This is done by shouting your bids and positioning your hands. Palms out means sell, palms in means buy. I can assure you it's a fun game to win.

Before I got into the grave-digging business I was a body-and-fender man. My job is more than grave-digging. It's maintenance and planning. It fills a need.

Construction King
CASE

I've been a diviner for fifty years. I've doodle-bugged for oil in Kansas, found water in Arizona and minerals in California. I've also looked for archeological sites, lost people and lost aeroplanes. Ninety percent of the time I find what I'm looking for.

My father came from Japan in the 1920's because America was the land of opportunity. During World War II we were interned in Utah and had to sacrifice the farm. It has taken thirty years to build up this vegetable farm to seventy acres with eleven men helping me. My son doesn't want to farm — it's hard work with little money. He works in the Blue Chip redemption center.

KRUGER & SONS
HOME OF THE HAPPY PICKLE
DO NOT CUT BELOW DOTTED LINE
4-1 GAL. PLASTIC JARS
UP

Catering truck drivers are mostly women. Men want to buy food from women, you know. I love being outdoors, getting around and meeting people. I'll never quit.

My dad always had a smile on his face so we named the company "Kruger & Sons, Home of the Happy Pickle." We are the most efficient pickle-packing plant on the West Coast, processing eight to ten million pounds of cucumbers each year. I started sorting pickles when I was ten years old. Dad would bring them home from work.

As long as I can work here, I will. It's better than housework. Cauliflower packing is hard work but I don't even think about it. My hands go through the motions, my mind's somewhere else. The season lasts six months, then I pack tomatoes and collect unemployment for the rest of the year.

To be a rice farmer you have to be good or you go under. You also have to be a lawyer, an accountant, an agronomist, a surveyor, a good mechanic and even-tempered. Our tractor is air-conditioned and has a radio. At the end of the day you know all the world news.

STEIGER

I take nude modeling seriously. It's hard to get jobs because so many people are ready to fling off their clothes. At first I felt awkward, but now moving comes naturally and my body falls into line. I'm not into parading nude at beaches.

The photographs in this book were taken with a Pentax 6x7 a Brooks Veriwide 2¼x3¼ and a Mamiya M645. All interior photographs were shot with Speed Graflex bare tubes, one for direct light and the other as fill-in. These portable lights give a soft natural light effect and are easy to handle. I shot 500 rolls of Tri-X 220 film, developed in Edwal FG-7 for ten minutes at 68°. All prints were made by Elliott Dopking in Livermore, California, and Chong Lee, San Francisco.